Copyright @ 2021 by John R. Brown and Brian J. Wright
ISBN: 978-1-5271-0699-4
Published by Christian Focus Publications Ltd
Geanies House, Fearn, Tain, Ross-shire IV20 1TW www.christianfocus.com

This edition published in 2021.
Cover illustration and internal illustrations by Lisa Flanagan
Cover and internal design by Lisa Flanagan
Printed and bound in Turkey

All rights reserved. No part of this publication may be reproduced, stored in a retrieval system, or transmitted, in any form, by any means, electronic, mechanical, photocopying, recording or otherwise without the prior permission of the publisher or a licence permitting restricted copying. In the U.K. such licences are issued by the Copyright Licensing Agency, 4 Battlebridge Lane, London, SE1 2HX. www.cla.co.uk

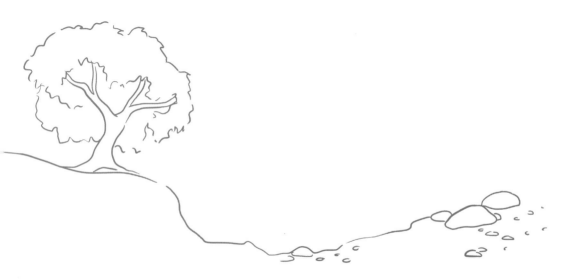

Zephaniah's hero

John Brown
Brian Wright

CF4·K

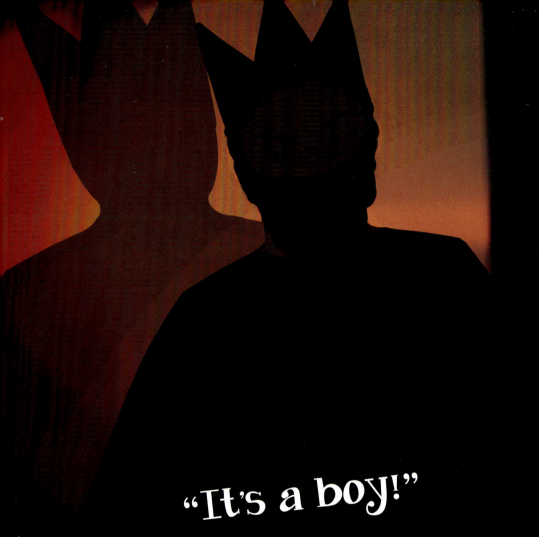

"It's a boy!"

The excited parents announced.

"And we're naming him Zephaniah—'the Lord hides'—because we're asking the good Lord to hide him from harm."

Zephaniah needed these prayers, for he was born during the dark, dangerous days of King Manasseh, who encouraged God's people to break God's rules.

When Zephaniah grew up, God sent him to warn his people that judgment was coming.

"**The Day of the Lord** is coming!
The day when the Lord judges the whole world!

In that day God will sweep away everything on earth,
like he did when he sent the flood in Noah's time."

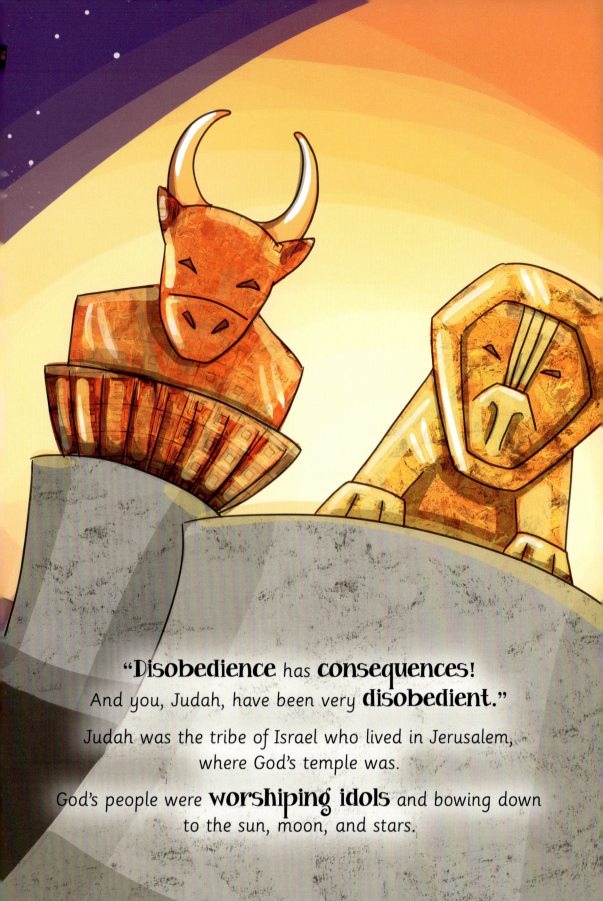

"**Disobedience** has **consequences!** And you, Judah, have been very **disobedient**."

Judah was the tribe of Israel who lived in Jerusalem, where God's temple was.

God's people were **worshiping idols** and bowing down to the sun, moon, and stars.

Judah **turned their back** on God
and refused to follow him.

They put on clothes to look like their neighbors,
who **worshiped false gods.**

They **followed strange superstitions,**
like hopping over the doorstep to the temple.

They took people's money by tricking and hurting them.

Isn't that sad?

Judah used to worship God and bow down to him. They used to obey his word and be nice to one another.

But Judah forgot that God was watching them
and didn't think he would punish them.

But they were wrong!

God sees everything we do and punishes every sin,
for he is holy.

God is also forgiving, though, so he sent Zephaniah to warn Judah.

"Change your ways, you lazybones, before I crush Jerusalem and knock down its walls!"

"I'll use my lantern to find whoever tries to hide, so don't think you can escape punishment!"

"If you want to escape punishment," Zephaniah said, "Then **tell God you're sorry** for disobeying him. Seek the Lord, seek humility, and seek righteousness."

To encourage Judah to seek God, Zephaniah warned them not to seek help from their neighbors—because God was going to judge them, too.

"Don't look to the **west**! God will judge the **Philistines**—Goliath's people—and knock down their cities! Don't look to the **east**! God will punish the **Moabites** and **Ammonites** and fill their land with nettles and salt pits!"

"Don't look to the **south!** God will punish the **Ethiopians** with his sword!"

"Don't look to the **north!** God will judge the **Assyrians,** and when he's done, their capital Ninevah will be empty except for some birds and wild animals!"

Then God reminded Jerusalem of their own rebellion. "Your **princes** are roaring lions! Your **judges** are hungry wolves! Your **prophets** lie, and your **priests** break my laws!"

The Lord sent Zephaniah to Judah so they would
turn away from their sins and come back to God.

God knew, however, that most people would ignore him.
And since he is righteous, he will judge them. But God is also
merciful, and he promised to **set all things right** some day.

"Wait patiently, my people,
for the time when judgment's **done**;
For I will purify all speech,
so all can worship me as **one**."

"My people will bring me gifts,
their loyalty to **prove**,
And none will feel ashamed,
for the rebels I'll **remove**."

"Their daytimes will be peaceful,
their sleep all sweet at **night**;
for gone will be all evil
that might scare or cause them **fright**."

"The Lord—your King—will live with you;
your troubles gone at **last**!
You'll never fear disaster again,
for your problems are all **past**."

"Your loving God will be with you,
a mighty hero who **saves!**
He will joyfully delight in you,
and sing over you with **praise!**"

"I will gather those whose hearts were sad, when my laws were **disobeyed.**"

"I will heal the sick, honor the shamed, and gather those chased **away.**"

"On that day I'll bring you home,
and all the world will **know**,
That I forgave you and put things right,
by the blessings I'll **bestow**."

We don't know when all this will happen, but we do know
the name of the Mighty Hero God is sending to save us...

Jesus!

Jesus came to rescue everyone who is sorry for doing bad and trusts in him as their Savior.

And Jesus is coming back again to bring all God's children home to live with him **forever!**

When you read Zephaniah, "the Lord hides," remember that
God hides from harm those who trust in him,
even when we've done bad things.

Praise God for sending Zephaniah! Praise God for sending Jesus!
Hallelujah! What a Savior!

Christian Focus Publications publishes books for adults and children under its four main imprints: Christian Focus, CF4K, Mentor and Christian Heritage. Our books reflect our conviction that God's Word is reliable and Jesus is the way to know him, and live for ever with him.

Our children's publication list covers pre-school to early teens. We also publish personal and family devotional titles, biographies and inspirational stories that children will love.

From pre-school board books to teenage apologetics, we have it covered!

"Why not just skip Zephaniah? Brian and John show us why—we might miss Jesus in the Minor Prophets. Zephaniah is not about a man by that name. It's about the gospel—God's grace in sending Jesus!"
BARBARA REAOCH, former director of the Children's Division of Bible Study Fellowship International, and author of *A Better Than Anything Christmas* and *A Jesus Christmas*

"Too many people--kids and parents included—miss out on the rich truths of the Minor Prophets. I am happy to recommend Zephaniah by Dr. Wright and Pastor Brown as a rich resource for families. This fresh look at an overlooked book will bless you and your children."
DIANNE JAGO, mother of three, founder of *Deeply Rooted Magazine*, and author of *A Holy Pursuit: How the Gospel Frees Us to Follow and Lay Down Our Dreams*

"In teaching our children, Christian parents and children's workers are always on the lookout for expressions of biblical truth that are clear, simple, and understandable. They do so with hopes and prayers that, in using these, our children will see more of the beauty of God and his word as they understand these better. What a joy and blessing to have now a resource that does just this with one of the parts of the Bible that may seem most distant for our children, but parts that, rightly understood, are tremendously relevant and life-impacting. Brian Wright and John Brown provide beautifully crafted and compelling renditions of the Minor Prophets in ways that we and our children can understand better the powerful message of these books of the Bible. They carefully uncover the ancient context of these messages while bringing them forward to our day, and in ways our children can understand. I have no doubt of the tremendous benefit these will prove to be for countless Christian parents and churches."
BRUCE A. WARE, Professor of Christian Theology, Southern Seminary, Louisville, Kentucky and author of *Big Truths for Young Hearts*

"The entire Bible, even the section called the Minor Prophets, is relevant for God's people, including children. Kudos to the authors for making the Minor Prophets accessible to children through these illustrated, engaging summaries of each of the twelve books. After reading these summaries, children should come away knowing what each book is about, as well as the important principles God wants us to learn. I'm looking forward to reading this book to my grandsons in the days ahead."
ROBERT CHISHOLM, Chair and Senior Professor of Old Testament Studies, Dallas Theological Seminary, and author of *Interpreting the Minor Prophets* and *Handbook on the Prophets*

Copyright @ 2021 by John R. Brown and Brian J. Wright
ISBN: 978-1-5271-0701-4
Published by Christian Focus Publications Ltd
Geanies House, Fearn, Tain, Ross-shire IV20 1TW www.christianfocus.com

This edition published in 2021.
Cover illustration and internal illustrations by Lisa Flanagan
Cover and internal design by Lisa Flanagan
Printed and bound in Turkey

All rights reserved. No part of this publication may be reproduced, stored in a retrieval system, or transmitted, in any form, by any means, electronic, mechanical, photocopying, recording or otherwise without the prior permission of the publisher or a licence permitting restricted copying. In the U.K. such licences are issued by the Copyright Licensing Agency, 4 Battlebridge Lane, London, SE1 2HX. www.cla.co.uk

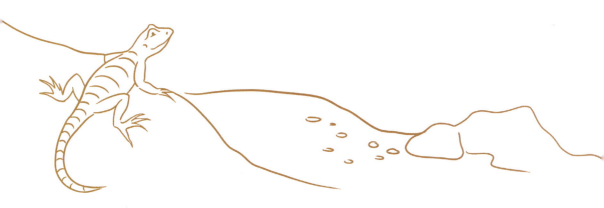

Obadiah
& the Edomites

John Brown
Brian Wright

CF4·K

His name means "the Lord's servant." He was **a prophet**, someone chosen by God to deliver **God's messages** to **God's people**.

One day God showed Obadiah how he was going to punish Israel's neighbors, **the Edomites.** The Edomites had been mean to God's people, Israel, for a **very long time.**

It all started with twin brothers named **Jacob** and **Esau.**

Esau was born first, which meant he would get more of the family's property. But when he grew up, he sold his bigger share to his younger brother, Jacob, for a bowl of **red stew**. This foolish trade earned him the nickname "Edom," which means **"Red,"** which is why his family were called the **Edomites.**

Jacob's family was called **Israel,** which was the new name God gave Jacob. The Edomites and Israelites lived next to each other, and **they fought** a lot!

The Israelites served **the one true God**, but the Edomites created their own gods. The Edomites refused to be nice to the Israelites, which made God very angry. He does not like it when people mistreat his children.

But the Edomites didn't care, for they lived in a rock fortress high in the mountains called **Petra**, **"the Rock"**! They boasted, "No one can get us way up here!"

They were wrong, though, for their pride deceived them.

So God warned them,

"Even if you lived **as high as eagles** fly,
as high as stars in the sky,
even from way up there
I will bring you **crashing down!**"

God had blessed the Edomites with a place to live, food to eat, and many good things to enjoy. But they weren't grateful. Instead **they rejected God** and mistreated his people.

But God gets angry when people do bad things. And the Edomites had been **very bad** for a **very long time.**

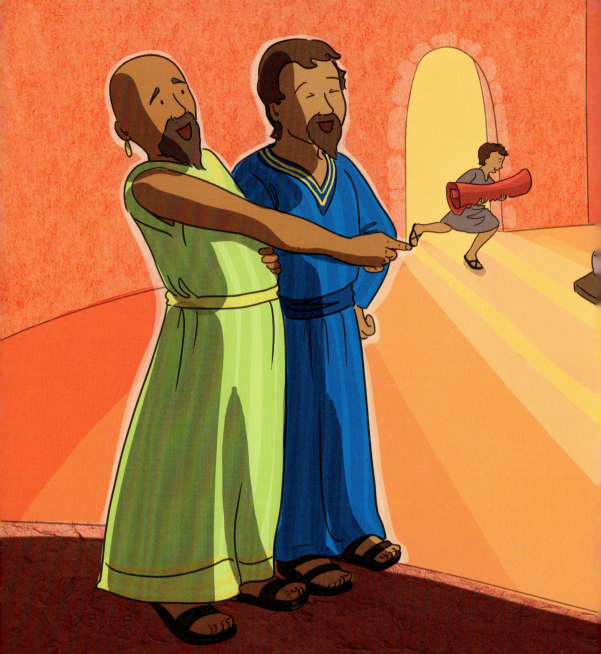

One time some mean people from Babylon (the same people who put Daniel's three friends in the fiery furnace) came to Israel and started **hurting God's people** and **stealing from God's temple.**

Did the Edomites come to help their relatives, the Israelites?

No! In fact, they laughed and made fun of them!

God wasn't laughing, though, and he told the Edomites to stop. But did they listen to God? **No!**
They kept on laughing and teasing. Then it got worse.

The Edomites started stealing from Israel! "Stop stealing!" God told the Edomites through Obadiah.

But did they listen to God? No!

They kept on stealing. Then it got even worse.

The Edomites started hurting the Israelites! The Edomites took God's children and gave them to mean people. "Stop hurting my children!" God told the Edomites through Obadiah.

But did they listen to God? **No!**

They kept on hurting his children.

Can you believe all the bad things the Edomites did?

First, **they refused** to protect their relatives the Israelites.

Then **they laughed** at them.

Then **they stole** from them.

Then **they hurt** them and **took them away** from their home!

Can you imagine how angry they made God? **Israel** had also made God angry, for they were disobeying him as well. Therefore God's message to the Edomites was a warning to **the Israelites** too.

Obadiah warned that the Edomites' **pride** would be their **downfall,** for God doesn't like it when we think we're better than we are—especially when this leads us to **ignore** or **disobey** God!

So to **humble them,** God said he would take away everyone they trusted in instead of him.

Their friends would betray them.

Their teachers would be destroyed.

Their soldiers would be defeated.

The Edomites were in **BIG** trouble!

Then Obadiah shared some **good news** with Israel.

One day God will punish all the bad people and keep them from hurting anyone ever again.

At that time, God will bring all his children home to live together with him forever.

Best of all,

God himself will be King in that day!
King Jesus is coming to judge and to rule!
Everything will be perfect when King Jesus
rules God's people in **God's kingdom!**

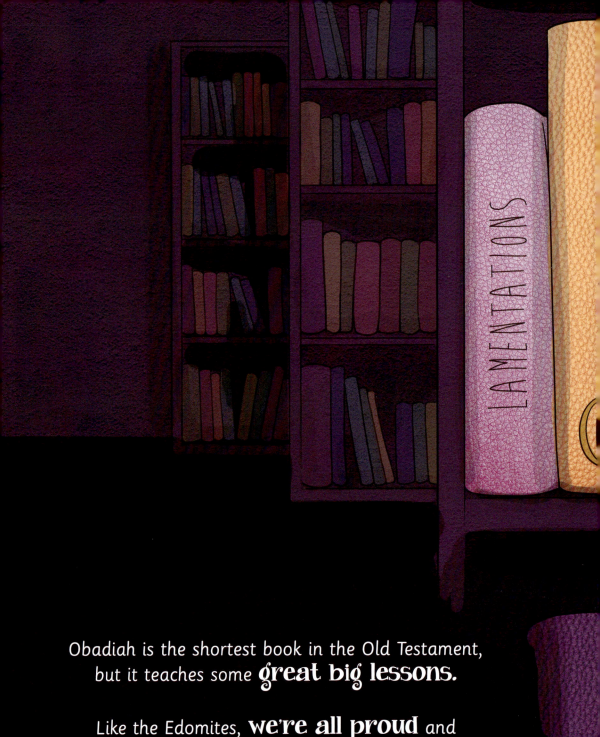

Obadiah is the shortest book in the Old Testament, but it teaches some **great big lessons.**

Like the Edomites, **we're all proud** and need to humble ourselves before God.

Like the Edomites and Israelites, **we've all done bad things** that make God angry.

But if we ask God to forgive us
and trust in **his Son, King Jesus,** to be **our Savior,**
then we'll live with God forever someday.

Amen!

Christian Focus Publications publishes books for adults and children under its four main imprints: Christian Focus, CF4K, Mentor and Christian Heritage. Our books reflect our conviction that God's Word is reliable and Jesus is the way to know him, and live for ever with him.

Our children's publication list covers pre-school to early teens. We also publish personal and family devotional titles, biographies and inspirational stories that children will love.

From pre-school board books to teenage apologetics, we have it covered!

"Have you thought Obadiah was too hard for kids to understand? With clarity and biblical truth about Jesus in the Minor Prophets, Brian and John will convince you otherwise."
> BARBARA REAOCH, former director of the Children's Division of Bible Study Fellowship International, and author of *A Better Than Anything Christmas* and *A Jesus Christmas*

"Too many people--kids and parents included—miss out on the rich truths of the Minor Prophets. I am happy to recommend Obadiah by Dr. Wright and Pastor Brown as a rich resource for families. This fresh look at an overlooked book will bless you and your children."
> DIANNE JAGO, mother of three, founder of *Deeply Rooted Magazine*, and author of *A Holy Pursuit: How the Gospel Frees Us to Follow and Lay Down Our Dreams*

"In teaching our children, Christian parents and children's workers are always on the lookout for expressions of biblical truth that are clear, simple, and understandable. They do so with hopes and prayers that, in using these, our children will see more of the beauty of God and his word as they understand these better. What a joy and blessing to have now a resource that does just this with one of the parts of the Bible that may seem most distant for our children, but parts that, rightly understood, are tremendously relevant and life-impacting. Brian Wright and John Brown provide beautifully crafted and compelling renditions of the Minor Prophets in ways that we and our children can understand better the powerful message of these books of the Bible. They carefully uncover the ancient context of these messages while bringing them forward to our day, and in ways our children can understand. I have no doubt of the tremendous benefit these will prove to be for countless Christian parents and churches."
> BRUCE A. WARE, Professor of Christian Theology, Southern Seminary, Louisville, Kentucky, and author of *Big Truths for Young Hearts*

"The entire Bible, even the section called the Minor Prophets, is relevant for God's people, including children. Kudos to the authors for making the Minor Prophets accessible to children through these illustrated, engaging summaries of each of the twelve books. After reading these summaries, children should come away knowing what each book is about, as well as the important principles God wants us to learn. I'm looking forward to reading this book to my grandsons in the days ahead."
> ROBERT CHISHOLM, Chair and Senior Professor of Old Testament Studies, Dallas Theological Seminary, and author of *Interpreting the Minor Prophets* and *Handbook on the Prophets*

Copyright @ 2021 by John R. Brown and Brian J. Wright
ISBN: 978-1-5271-0700-7
Published by Christian Focus Publications Ltd
Geanies House, Fearn, Tain, Ross-shire IV20 1TW www.christianfocus.com

This edition published in 2021.
Cover illustration and internal illustrations by Lisa Flanagan
Cover and internal design by Lisa Flanagan
Printed and bound in Turkey

All rights reserved. No part of this publication may be reproduced, stored in a retrieval system, or transmitted, in any form, by any means, electronic, mechanical, photocopying, recording or otherwise without the prior permission of the publisher or a licence permitting restricted copying. In the U.K. such licences are issued by the Copyright Licensing Agency, 4 Battlebridge Lane, London, SE1 2HX. www.cla.co.uk

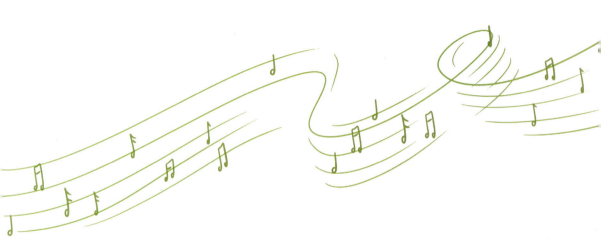

Habakkuk's Song

John Brown
Brian Wright

CF4•K

Long ago, **God's people Israel** were breaking God's rules.

God said, "Don't worship false gods." But they did.

God said, "Love one another." But they didn't.

God said, "Repent!" But they wouldn't.

This made **Habakkuk,** one of God's chosen prophets, really upset. He was so upset that he cried out to God.

"Help!"

"Bad people are hurting others everywhere! Aren't you going to do anything about it? Aren't you listening to me? How long are you going to let this go on?"

These were **bold questions!**

But did God get angry at Habakkuk? No, because he knew Habakkuk's heart. And God was about to do something about all the bad things mean people were doing.

"**Look,** Habakkuk, and **be amazed!**

I'm sending **the Babylonians** to punish Israel right now! They're coming faster than cheetahs, fiercer than wolves, like an eagle swooping down on its prey!" "They'll blow through the land like the wind and take my disobedient people away."

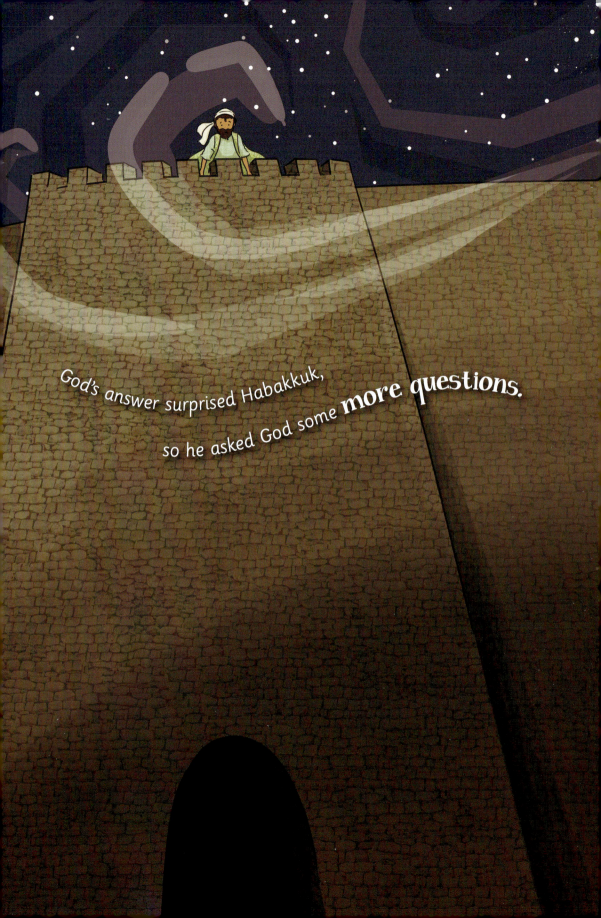

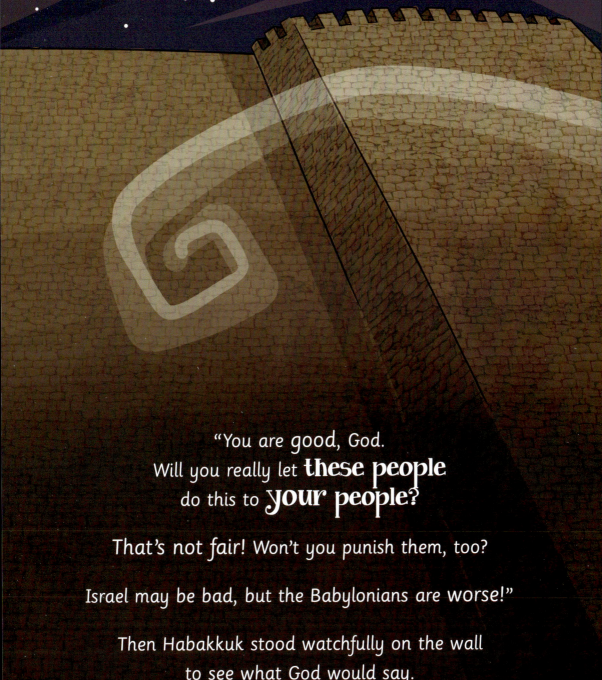

"You are good, God.
Will you really let **these people**
do this to **your people?**

That's not fair! Won't you punish them, too?

Israel may be bad, but the Babylonians are worse!"

Then Habakkuk stood watchfully on the wall
to see what God would say.

"**Write this down** in your best handwriting," said the Lord, "so messengers can deliver my message on tablets for everyone to read."

"Someday I will punish selfish, greedy, and dishonest people. I will punish those who hurt others, who worship false gods, and who make others do bad things. Certainly, I will punish everyone who does bad."

"I will **punish** the arrogant Babylonians, who kidnapped their neighbors and stole their stuff."

"So **don't be like them!** People who are proud are wicked, but those who trust in the Lord are righteous."

Then **God** gave Habakkuk **five songs** warning how bad it would be for the Babylonians when God punished them.

"**How bad it will be** for you Babylonians, who hurt your neighbors and stole their stuff."

"**How bad it will be** for you Babylonians, who built your homes with money you stole from people you hurt!"

"**How bad it will be** for you Babylonians, who built your city with stolen money you got by violence! For God will burn your wicked cities down!"

"Indeed, the Lord will make all wicked nations like you disappear;
For the whole earth will know how great God is, like water covering the sea."

"How bad it will be for you Babylonians, who mistreat your neighbors and make them do bad things!"

God will punish them for everything! He'll make them drink the cup of his wrath down to the very last drop!

"**How bad it will be** for you Babylonians, who make idols that aren't alive and can't talk."

"**But the Lord** is alive, and he's in his holy temple, so let all the earth be quiet before him!"

After writing down God's five songs,
Habakkuk wrote **a song of his own.**

It was a song praising God for how wonderful he is
and for all he's done for his children.

"I've heard about you, Lord,

and am awed by all you **do.**

Please save us in our need,

and your mercy now **renew."**

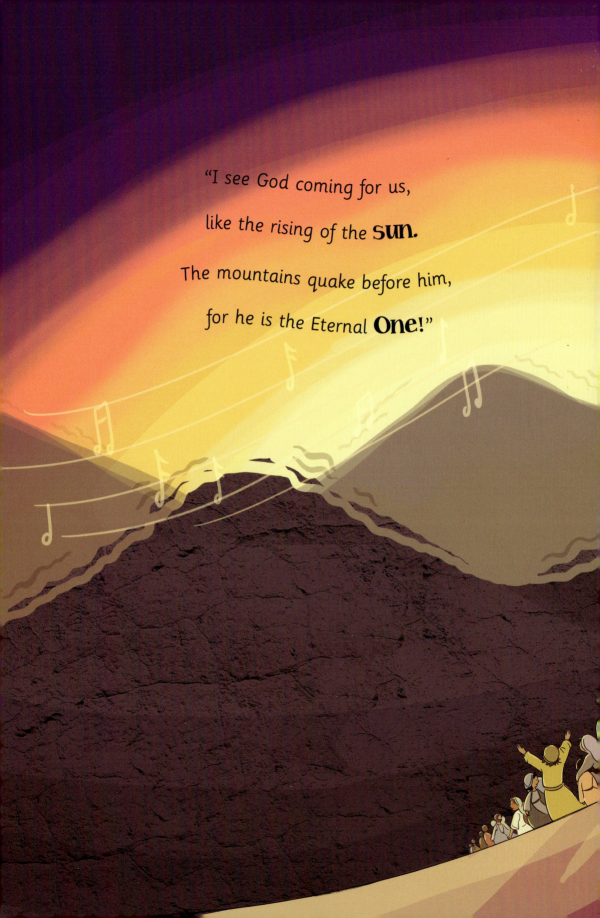
"I see God coming for us, like the rising of the **sun**. The mountains quake before him, for he is the Eternal **One**!"

"You rescued Israel from Egypt,

with your mighty chariots and **bow**.

And soon you'll crush your enemies,

just like you did **Pharaoh**."

"You go forth to save Your people,

and your Anointed **One**.

For you crush the head of the wicked,

and victory is **won**."

"Now I wait in frightened silence,

for the day you come to **judge**.

But even if all my blessings leave,

my joy in you won't **budge**!"

Our strength is still the Sovereign Lord,

whose saving name we **hymn!**

Righteous people trust Christ the Lord,

and live by faith in **him.**

Christian Focus Publications publishes books for adults and children under its four main imprints: Christian Focus, CF4K, Mentor and Christian Heritage. Our books reflect our conviction that God's Word is reliable and Jesus is the way to know him, and live for ever with him.

Our children's publication list covers pre-school to early teens. We also publish personal and family devotional titles, biographies and inspirational stories that children will love.

From pre-school board books to teenage apologetics, we have it covered!

"Why do bad things happen? Habakkuk struggled to understand this — your kids will, too! With simply-stated biblical truths, Brian and John show us Habakkuk's trust in God and points us to Jesus who came to rescue us from a greater evil — our sin."
BARBARA REAOCH, former director of the Children's Division of Bible Study Fellowship International, and author of *A Better Than Anything Christmas* and *A Jesus Christmas*

"Too many people—kids and parents included—miss out on the rich truths of the Minor Prophets. I am happy to recommend Habakkuk by Dr. Wright and Pastor Brown as a rich resource for families. This fresh look at an overlooked book will bless you and your children."
DIANNE JAGO, mother of three, founder of *Deeply Rooted Magazine*, and author of *A Holy Pursuit: How the Gospel Frees Us to Follow and Lay Down Our Dreams*

"In teaching our children, Christian parents and children's workers are always on the lookout for expressions of biblical truth that are clear, simple, and understandable. They do so with hopes and prayers that, in using these, our children will see more of the beauty of God and his word as they understand these better. What a joy and blessing to have now a resource that does just this with one of the parts of the Bible that may seem most distant for our children, but parts that, rightly understood, are tremendously relevant and life-impacting. Brian Wright and John Brown provide beautifully crafted and compelling renditions of the Minor Prophets in ways that we and our children can understand better the powerful message of these books of the Bible. They carefully uncover the ancient context of these messages while bringing them forward to our day, and in ways our children can understand. I have no doubt of the tremendous benefit these will prove to be for countless Christian parents and churches."
BRUCE A. WARE, Professor of Christian Theology, Southern Seminary, Louisville, Kentucky, and author of *Big Truths for Young Hearts*

"The entire Bible, even the section called the Minor Prophets, is relevant for God's people, including children. Kudos to the authors for making the Minor Prophets accessible to children through these illustrated, engaging summaries of each of the twelve books. After reading these summaries, children should come away knowing what each book is about, as well as the important principles God wants us to learn. I'm looking forward to reading this book to my grandsons in the days ahead."
ROBERT CHISHOLM, Chair and Senior Professor of Old Testament Studies, Dallas Theological Seminary, and author of *Interpreting the Minor Prophets* and *Handbook on the Prophets*

Copyright @ 2021 by John R. Brown and Brian J. Wright
ISBN: 978-1-5271-0702-1
Published by Christian Focus Publications Ltd
Geanies House, Fearn, Tain, Ross-shire IV20 1TW www.christianfocus.com

This edition published in 2021.
Cover illustration and internal illustrations by Lisa Flanagan
Cover and internal design by Lisa Flanagan
Printed and bound in Turkey

All rights reserved. No part of this publication may be reproduced, stored in a retrieval system, or transmitted, in any form, by any means, electronic, mechanical, photocopying, recording or otherwise without the prior permission of the publisher or a licence permitting restricted copying. In the U.K. such licences are issued by the Copyright Licensing Agency, 4 Battlebridge Lane, London, SE1 2HX. www.cla.co.uk

The dates of Haggai's messages have been converted by Bible scholars and historians to correspond to modern calendars. They remind us that Haggai was a real person who really spoke these words to God's people on these specific days.

Haggai's feast

John Brown
Brian Wright

CF4·K

Haggai's name means **"feast,"** but the feasts weren't very festive in Haggai's day.

You see, Israel had stopped building **God's temple.**

So God stopped the **rain,**

which stopped the **crops,**

which left the people **hungry,**

and **thirsty.**

So God sent his prophet Haggai to tell his people to **get busy building** his temple.

Why did God's temple need rebuilding? Because Israel had been **very bad** for a **very long time.**

So God sent a wicked nation to knock down his temple and take the Israelites **far, far away.**

But God is very good and very forgiving, so after a long time, he brought his people **home again.**

When they got home, God told them, "Rebuild my temple first, then you can work on your own houses and farms."

So they did ... for a while.

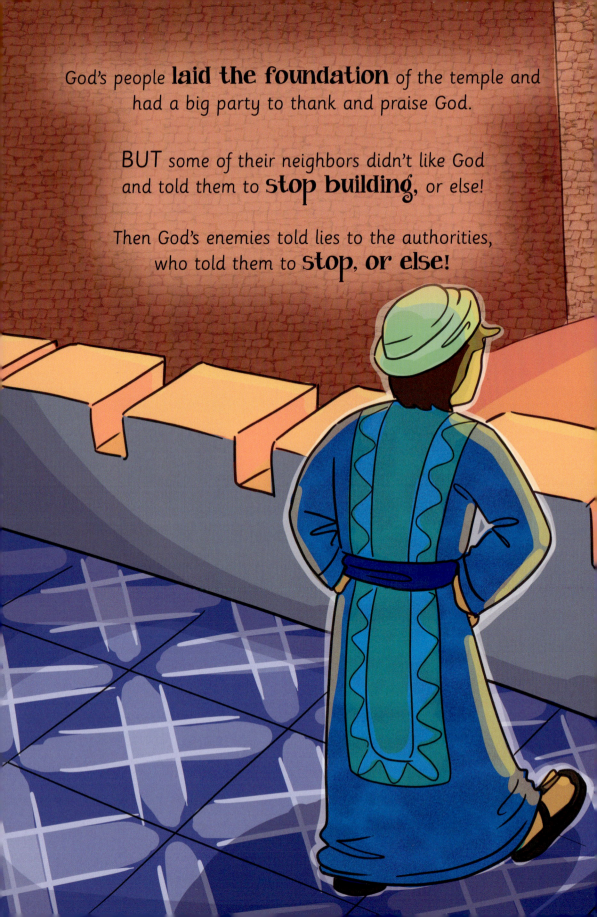

So Israel disobeyed God and **stopped rebuilding** his temple like he told them.

Instead, they **built fancy homes** for themselves and started farming their own land. They forgot about God and **did what they wanted**, which was a really, really bad idea.

And so ...

They planted **much** but harvested **little**.

They drank **a lot** but stayed **thirsty**.

They dressed **warm**,
but stayed **cold.**

They worked **hard**
but had **no money.**

Then the rain **stopped**
and the crops **died**.

God was teaching them a lesson.
"Disobeying me is always a really, really bad idea."

That's when God sent Haggai to deliver **five messages** on **four days.**

On **August 29,** Haggai delivered his **first message** to the governor and the high priest.

"God says, 'Tell my people to **get back to work** rebuilding my temple!'"

So God's children started building again, and God started blessing them again. God was teaching his children that we can only be **happy** when we **obey** him.

Haggai's **second message** came on **September 21** during Israel's autumn harvest feast.

"'**I am with you**,' says the Lord!"

This made everyone so happy that they finished the temple in less than a month!

Three weeks after that, on **October 17**, Haggai delivered his **third message.**

"Who remembers the first temple before it got knocked down? It was bigger and better than this new one, wasn't it?"

"But don't be sad; **be strong!** Someday God will live in this temple and make everything wonderful everywhere!"

Haggai delivered his **last two messages** on December 18.

"If your hands are dirty, anything you touch gets dirty, right? Well, you've made everything dirty by disobeying me. This is why you never had enough food, water, money, or warmth.

But now that you've started obeying me again, **I will bless you.**"

Haggai's **last message** was the best of all.

"Someday I will get rid of your enemies and establish my **Forever King**. I, the Lord of the angel armies, have spoken!"

When Haggai got to **heaven**, he learned **something special** you may already know...

This Forever King is none other than God's own Son,
Jesus Christ!

The King came to earth at **Christmas**, died on **Good Friday,** and came back to life on **Easter** so that we could live with God in heaven, too.

All we have to do is be truly sorry for our sins
and trust in Jesus alone to save us.
This can be done by a prayer like this,
if you really mean it!

"God, I've done bad things, and I'm sorry.
I believe that Jesus is your Son,
and that he died for me on the cross.
So please forgive me and
let me serve King Jesus from now on.

Amen."

Although Haggai delivered his **five messages** long ago, they still apply to us today.

Don't disobey God, for he disciplines the disobedient.

Be brave, for God is with us.

Stand strong, for God is coming.

Obey God,
for he blesses
the obedient.

Trust and obey
King Jesus,
for he is God's
Forever King!

Christian Focus Publications publishes books for adults and children under its four main imprints: Christian Focus, CF4K, Mentor and Christian Heritage. Our books reflect our conviction that God's Word is reliable and Jesus is the way to know him, and live for ever with him.

Our children's publication list covers pre-school to early teens. We also publish personal and family devotional titles, biographies and inspirational stories that children will love.

From pre-school board books to teenage apologetics, we have it covered!

CF4•K
Because you're never too young to know Jesus

"Why teach Haggai to your kids? Open this book and see the clear and simple truths that Brian and John share from this not so minor prophet. God's Forever King is coming—His name is Jesus!"
BARBARA REAOCH, former director of the Children's Division of Bible Study Fellowship International, and author of *A Better Than Anything Christmas* and *A Jesus Christmas*

"Too many people—kids and parents included—miss out on the rich truths of the Minor Prophets. I am happy to recommend Habakkuk by Dr. Wright and Pastor Brown as a rich resource for families. This fresh look at an overlooked book will bless you and your children."
DIANNE JAGO, mother of three, founder of *Deeply Rooted Magazine*, and author of *A Holy Pursuit: How the Gospel Frees Us to Follow and Lay Down Our Dreams*

"In teaching our children, Christian parents and children's workers are always on the lookout for expressions of biblical truth that are clear, simple, and understandable. They do so with hopes and prayers that, in using these, our children will see more of the beauty of God and his word as they understand these better. What a joy and blessing to have now a resource that does just this with one of the parts of the Bible that may seem most distant for our children, but parts that, rightly understood, are tremendously relevant and life-impacting. Brian Wright and John Brown provide beautifully crafted and compelling renditions of the Minor Prophets in ways that we and our children can understand better the powerful message of these books of the Bible. They carefully uncover the ancient context of these messages while bringing them forward to our day, and in ways our children can understand. I have no doubt of the tremendous benefit these will prove to be for countless Christian parents and churches."
BRUCE A. WARE, Professor of Christian Theology, Southern Seminary, Louisville, Kentucky, and author of *Big Truths for Young Hearts*

"The entire Bible, even the section called the Minor Prophets, is relevant for God's people, including children. Kudos to the authors for making the Minor Prophets accessible to children through these illustrated, engaging summaries of each of the twelve books. After reading these summaries, children should come away knowing what each book is about, as well as the important principles God wants us to learn. I'm looking forward to reading this book to my grandsons in the days ahead."
ROBERT CHISHOLM, Chair and Senior Professor of Old Testament Studies, Dallas Theological Seminary, and author of *Interpreting the Minor Prophets* and *Handbook on the Prophets*